Voyeurism Unv

A Deep Dive into Faceless YouTube Channels

By Ben Davis

Contents

Chapter 1: The Origins of Faceless YouTube Channels

As the internet continues to evolve, new forms of content and entertainment emerge, captivating online communities in unique and unexpected ways. One such phenomenon that has gained tremendous popularity in recent years is the faceless YouTube channel. These channels, shrouded in mystery and anonymity, have captivated audiences worldwide, leaving them intrigued and hungry for more.

To truly understand the origins of faceless YouTube channels, we must delve into their humble beginnings. At the onset, the online landscape primarily consisted of individuals sharing personal stories, documenting their lives, and showcasing their talents. However, a subtle shift took place, fueling the rise of faceless YouTube channels. Creators began to realize the power of anonymity, realizing that it could capture the imagination and curiosity of viewers in unprecedented ways.

The first inklings of faceless channels emerged in the early 2010s. Pioneers like "The Mysterious Pen" and "Unknown Vlogger" were among the first to experiment with this concept. By obscuring their identities behind masks, voice modulations, or simply by never showing their faces, these creators tapped into a primal human instinct – the allure of the mysterious and unknown.

Intriguingly, faceless YouTube channels ignited debates regarding the authenticity of content creation. Critics argued that these mysterious creators were mere attention-seekers, leveraging anonymity as a cheap tactic to increase viewership. However, supporters saw it differently. They believed that faceless channels allowed creators to focus solely on the content without the distractions that often come with revealing one's identity. It allowed the audience to focus purely on the message being conveyed.

The emergence of faceless YouTube channels also coincided with the growing popularity of horror and suspense genres. Creators like "The Enigma" and "Shadow Master" began crafting gripping narrative-driven series, utilizing anonymity to evoke a sense of unease and anticipation. The faceless personas they assumed became characters in their own right, adding depth and intrigue to their content.

As these channels gained traction, the creators faced a dilemma: embrace their newfound fame and reveal their identities or remain in the shadows. Surprisingly, many chose the latter. Maintaining anonymity became a hallmark of the faceless YouTube channel genre, captivating audiences further with the enigma surrounding the creators' true identities.

With each passing year, faceless YouTube channels evolved. Creators developed distinct styles, refining their storytelling techniques and enhancing the production value of their content. Some adopted signature motifs, such as eerie background music or cryptic symbols, leaving viewers on the edge of their seats, eagerly awaiting each new upload.

The rise of faceless YouTube channels holds a mirror to our fascination with the unknown. In an internet era dominated by oversharing and self-promotion, these channels provide a refreshing break from the status quo. They tap into our innate curiosity and ignite our imagination, reminding us that, sometimes, what we don't know can be more compelling than what we do.

As we explore the history and development of faceless YouTube channels, we uncover a captivating world of mystery, suspense, and boundless creativity. In the second half of this chapter, we will delve deeper into the impact of faceless channels on the online community, as well as the psychological factors that contribute to their enduring allure. Stay tuned for an eye-opening examination of this enigmatic phenomenon!

In the second half of this chapter, we delve deeper into the impact of faceless YouTube channels on the online community, as well as the psychological factors that contribute to their enduring allure. The emergence of these enigmatic creators has not only transformed the content landscape but has also sparked intriguing discussions within the online community.

One significant impact of faceless YouTube channels is their ability to connect with viewers on a deeper emotional level. By remaining faceless, these creators tap into a universal fear of the unknown, creating a sense of mystery and suspense that keeps audiences coming back for more. The anonymized personas they adopt become vessels for storytelling, allowing for immersive experiences that ignite the imagination of viewers.

Psychologically, faceless YouTube channels play into our innate desire to solve mysteries and unravel complex narratives. As humans, we are hardwired to seek answers and make sense of the world around us. These channels provide a unique form of entertainment that challenges our perception and engages our critical thinking skills. We find ourselves piecing together clues and speculating on the true identity of these creators, fueling a sense of intrigue and intellectual stimulation.

Furthermore, faceless YouTube channels have fostered a sense of community among their dedicated fans. Viewers often come together in online forums and discussion boards, sharing theories, dissecting plotlines, and supporting their favorite creators. The anonymity of these channels allows individuals from diverse backgrounds and walks of life to connect solely through the shared experience of watching and analyzing content, fostering a sense of camaraderie and belonging within the online space.

One curious aspect surrounding faceless YouTube channels is the ongoing debate regarding their authenticity. Critics argue that these creators hide behind anonymity as a gimmick, relying on secrecy to generate hype and attract viewers. However, supporters contest that anonymity allows for pure content creation, divorced from the distractions and biases that can come with personal identities. It is in this tension between authenticity and anonymity that the true power of faceless YouTube channels lies, pushing both creators and viewers to question the role of identity in the online realm.

As the popularity of faceless YouTube channels continues to grow, creators have pushed the boundaries of storytelling, incorporating immersive techniques and innovative production values. The use of visual effects, haunting sound design, and intricate storylines has propelled the genre to new heights. Viewers eagerly anticipate each new upload, eager to unravel the next layer of the narrative tapestry that these creators skillfully weave.

In conclusion, faceless YouTube channels have emerged as a captivating phenomenon within the online community, captivating audiences with their mysterious allure. As we explore their history and development, we uncover a realm of boundless creativity, suspense, and imagination. These channels not only provide a refreshing escape from the oversharing culture but also tap into our fascination with the unknown. They challenge our perceptions, foster community, and provide an enticing alternative to conventional content creation. So join us as we continue our unravelling of the world of faceless YouTube channels, shedding light on the enigmatic nature of these anonymous creators and the enduring impact they have on online culture. Stay tuned for more captivating insights into this fascinating realm of online entertainment.

Chapter 2: Understanding Voyeurism in the Digital Age

As technology advances and our lives become increasingly interconnected, the concept of voyeurism has taken on a new dimension in the digital age. Online platforms have opened a window into the private lives of individuals, allowing us to observe and experience a world once hidden behind closed doors. This chapter delves into the psychological and sociological implications of voyeurism in the context of these faceless YouTube channels, exploring the fascination and consequences that arise from such behavior.

Voyeurism, at its core, is the act of deriving pleasure or gratification from watching others without their knowledge or consent. In the digital realm, it manifests itself through anonymous YouTube channels, where individuals capture and share footage of their daily lives. The allure lies in the sense of exclusivity, the idea that we, as viewers, are granted access to intimate moments that would otherwise remain unseen. This clandestine experience taps into our innate curiosity and need for new and exciting stimuli.

From a psychological standpoint, voyeurism provides a unique form of escapism. These faceless YouTube channels offer a safe space where viewers can temporarily disengage from their own lives and immerse themselves in the lives of others. The ability to vicariously experience different realities, relationships, and adventures allows individuals to explore alternative narratives and fulfill unmet desires. However, this escape comes at a cost.

As we venture deeper into the world of voyeurism, ethical concerns invariably surface. The consent and privacy of those being observed are compromised, raising questions about the boundaries of online ethics and the potential harm caused by such practices. The subjects of these YouTube channels might perpetuate the voyeuristic cycle by willingly sharing glimpses of their lives, but do they truly understand the implications? Are they fully aware of the impact it can have on their mental and emotional well-being? Furthermore, voyeurism in the digital age gives rise to blurred lines between reality and performance. As viewers, we often develop a parasocial relationship with the individuals we observe, feeling connected to their lives despite the absence of genuine interaction. This fabricated intimacy can lead to voyeuristic behaviors evolving into obsession or even stalking, blurring the boundaries between innocent fascination and unhealthy fixation.

Sociologically, voyeurism on online platforms is a reflection of our ever-evolving society. As we navigate a world that increasingly relies on screens for communication and connection, these channels provide a glimpse into the complexities of modern life. They offer a forum of shared experiences, allowing viewers to collectively dissect and discuss the content, ultimately shaping societal norms and values.

In conclusion, the concept of voyeurism has transformed in the digital age, fueled by the allure of exclusive access and an intrinsic desire for escapism. Yet, as we venture deeper into this realm, ethical dilemmas emerge, questioning the impact on both the observed and the observer. This first half of the chapter has set the stage for a more profound exploration of the psychological and sociological implications of voyeurism—a journey that shall uncover the effects, potential dangers, and the blurred lines between reality and performance. Stay tuned for the second half, where we dive even deeper into this captivating realm of faceless YouTube channels.The second half of this chapter will delve even deeper into the psychological and sociological implications of voyeurism in the digital age, shedding light on the effects, potential dangers, and the blurred lines between reality and performance.

When it comes to the psychological impact of voyeurism, it is essential to consider the long-term consequences for both the observed and the observer. For the individuals who willingly share glimpses of their lives on these faceless YouTube channels, there may be a sense of validation and social validation that comes with having an audience. However, they may not fully comprehend the potential harm it can have on their mental and emotional well-being. It is crucial to recognize that the act of observing without consent violates personal boundaries and can lead to feelings of objectification and exploitation.

On the flip side, viewers who indulge in voyeuristic behaviors may find themselves caught in a cycle where their interest evolves into obsession or even stalking. This fabricated intimacy can blur the lines between innocent fascination and unhealthy fixation. As viewers become emotionally invested in the lives of those they observe, it becomes crucial to remind ourselves of the line between genuine connection and voyeuristic tendencies.

From a sociological standpoint, these faceless YouTube channels mirror our evolving society's complexities and provide a platform for shared experiences and discussions. They shape societal norms and values by collectively dissecting and reflecting upon the content presented. However, it is essential to maintain a critical lens and ensure that the discussions remain respectful and ethical.

As we navigate this digital age, it becomes increasingly important to address the ethical concerns surrounding voyeurism in online platforms. The consent and privacy of those observed should always be paramount, and practices that exploit or violate these rights must be firmly condemned.

Education and awareness play a crucial role in mitigating the potential dangers of voyeurism in the digital age. By fostering discussions and cultivating a better understanding of the psychological and sociological implications, we can strive for a society that respects personal boundaries, prioritizes consent, and ensures the well-being of all individuals involved.

In conclusion, analyzing voyeurism in the context of online platforms allows us to explore its psychological and sociological implications. It is vital to recognize the allure of exclusive access and escapism that fuel our fascination with faceless YouTube channels.

However, as we venture deeper into this realm, ethical dilemmas arise, questioning the impact on both the observed and the observer.

This second half of the chapter has ventured into a more profound exploration of the effects, potential dangers, and the blurred lines between reality and performance. As adults in the digital age, it is our responsibility to critically examine and understand the implications of voyeurism, striving for a more ethical and respectful online environment.

So, with a deeper understanding of the complexity surrounding voyeurism in the digital age, let us reflect and examine our own behaviors and attitudes towards online platforms, always considering the well-being and consent of others. Only through thoughtful reflection and nuanced discussions can we navigate this captivating realm of faceless YouTube channels and the wider online landscape.

Chapter 3: The Appeal of Faceless YouTubers

Delve into the reasons why faceless YouTube channels captivate audiences, unraveling the allure of their anonymity and intrigue.

In an era of endless content and boundless self-exposure, faceless YouTube channels have emerged as a captivating phenomenon. With thousands of creators donning masks, blurring their faces, or simply opting to stay out of the frame altogether, they have managed to amass millions of dedicated followers. But what is it about these enigmatic figures that enthralls audiences? Why do anonymous YouTubers hold such sway in the digital realm?

One aspect that contributes to the appeal of faceless YouTubers is the allure of anonymity. In a world where personal information is shared fiercely and obsessively, these channels offer a refreshing break from the norm. This anonymity creates a mystique around the creator, leaving the audience intrigued and hungry for more. Viewers are drawn to the idea of engaging with content that transcends the individual and focuses solely on the message.

The anonymity also serves as a blank canvas upon which viewers can project their own ideas and interpretations. Without the distraction of a recognizable face, the emphasis shifts onto the content itself, allowing for a more immersive experience. It becomes an escape, as the viewers detach from the creator's personal identity and immerse themselves in the ideas, stories, or challenges presented by the faceless figure on the screen.

Another factor that drives the appeal of faceless YouTubers is the element of intrigue. The unknown aspect invites curiosity and invites speculation. Who are these creators? What stories lie behind their shrouded identities? The lack of visual cues fuels a sense of mystery, encouraging viewers to actively engage in the content and be a part of the ongoing narrative.

Additionally, faceless YouTubers often embody certain archetypes or personas that resonate with their audience. They might adopt a superhero persona, becoming a symbol of hope and justice. Others might take on the role of a wise sage, offering guidance and wisdom without the distractions of their personal lives. This allows viewers to form a deeper emotional connection with the content, as they project their own desires and aspirations onto these faceless avatars.

Moreover, faceless YouTubers create a sense of universality through their anonymity. By removing their personal identities from the equation, they transcend gender, race, and cultural boundaries. This universal appeal allows a diverse range of individuals to relate to their content and find solace in the shared experiences and messages.

As we explore the world of faceless YouTubers, it becomes evident that their anonymity and intrigue are what captivate audiences. The allure of escaping into a content-driven realm, the thrill of uncovering the unknown, and the connection forged through archetypes all contribute to the phenomenon. In the second half of this chapter, we will delve deeper into specific examples and analyze the psychological factors that underpin the widespread popularity of faceless YouTube channels. Prepare yourself for a unique exploration into the untold stories of these enigmatic creators.One of the key psychological factors that contributes to the widespread appeal of faceless YouTube channels is the element of suspense. These enigmatic creators often master the art of leaving their viewers on the edge of their seats, eagerly anticipating the next installment or revelation. By crafting a narrative that slowly unravels over time, they create a sense of anticipation and excitement that keeps audiences hooked.

Take, for example, the faceless YouTuber known as "The Masked Storyteller." With each video, this mysterious figure presents gripping stories that leave viewers yearning for more. The absence of a visible face allows the focus to shift solely onto the story being told, enhancing the immersive experience. As viewers become invested in the narrative, they eagerly await the next chapter, craving closure and resolution.

In addition to suspense, faceless YouTubers often tap into the power of shared experiences. By shrouding their personal identities and appearing as a faceless figure, these creators transcend individual circumstances and become relatable to a wide range of viewers. This universality allows viewers to connect with the content on a deeper level, finding solace and connection in the shared experiences and messages conveyed.

An excellent example of this is the faceless YouTuber known as "The Masked Philosopher." Through the lens of philosophical discussions, this creator explores life's fundamental questions, providing insights and perspectives that resonate with viewers from all walks of life. By removing personal identity, the focus remains on the ideas and concepts presented, fostering an inclusive and thought-provoking environment.

Furthermore, faceless YouTubers often tap into the psychological phenomenon of projection. The facelessness of these creators invites viewers to imprint their own desires, fears, and experiences onto the content. When viewers project themselves onto these faceless avatars, they develop a deeper emotional connection, as they see aspects of themselves embodied by these enigmatic figures.

A striking example of this is the faceless YouTuber known as "The Anonymous Activist." This creator advocates for social justice, showcasing the struggles of marginalized communities and inspiring viewers to take action. By adopting a faceless persona, The Anonymous Activist becomes a symbol of collective empowerment. Viewers are prompted to project their own desires for change and equality onto this anonymous figure, creating a sense of unity and shared purpose.

As we delve deeper into the world of faceless YouTubers, it becomes clear that their appeal lies not only in their anonymity and mystery, but also in the psychological factors they engage to captivate audiences. The ability to generate suspense, create shared experiences, and evoke projection all contribute to the allure of these enigmatic creators. In conclusion, faceless YouTube channels have become a captivating phenomenon due to their ability to offer a refreshing break from the norm of self-exposure and the allure of anonymity. By detaching personal identity and focusing solely on the content, they provide an immersive escape for viewers. The element of intrigue, projection of archetypes, and the universality they embody further contribute to their widespread popularity. As we continue to uncover the untold stories of these enigmatic creators, we gain a deeper understanding of the psychological factors that underpin their appeal. Stay tuned for a unique exploration into the intriguing world of faceless YouTubers.

Chapter 4: Ethical Considerations in Faceless YouTube Channel Creation

In the virtual realm of YouTube, a peculiar subset of content creators has risen to prominence - faceless YouTube channels. These channels, often shrouded in mystery and anonymity, have captivated millions of viewers around the world. Yet, behind the allure lies a complex web of ethical considerations that demand our attention. As we explore the realm of faceless YouTube channel creation, it becomes essential to confront the ethical dilemmas associated with both creating and consuming such content.

One of the foremost concerns is the impact on privacy. Faceless YouTube channels rely on remaining anonymous, allowing creators to protect their identity while documenting their experiences or sharing their knowledge. However, this anonymity can also encroach upon the privacy of others. By capturing unsuspecting individuals in their videos without obtaining explicit consent, faceless creators may inadvertently breach their subjects' right to privacy. This raises questions about the boundaries between public and private spaces when it comes to online content creation. At what point does the desire for exclusive content supersede the rights of individuals to privacy?

Furthermore, the act of consuming faceless YouTube content brings its own ethical dilemmas. As viewers, we become voyeurs, surreptitiously observing the lives and experiences of others. The appeal of faceless channels lies in the curiosity they evoke, as we listen to their stories or immerse ourselves in their adventures. However, this curiosity can blur the line between harmless entertainment and voyeurism. The popularity of these channels rests on our collective willingness to invade the private lives of others, prompting us to question the role of consent and the responsibility of both creators and viewers.

One argument raised in defense of faceless YouTube channels is that they provide a platform for marginalized voices to be heard. By removing the focus from their physical appearance, creators can share their stories without facing potential bias or discrimination based on their race, gender, or other personal attributes. This unique form of expression can challenge societal norms and serve as a catalyst for dialogue and understanding. However, even with good intentions, it is crucial to recognize the potential drawbacks and unintended consequences that come with this form of content creation.

As we navigate this fascinating and controversial realm, it is essential to tread carefully. Both creators and viewers must consider the potential consequences and ethical implications of their actions. Respect for privacy and consent should form the foundation upon which faceless YouTube content is built. Striking a balance between providing a platform for diverse voices and preserving individual rights is key to ensuring the responsible creation and consumption of such content.

The continued exploration of ethical considerations surrounding faceless YouTube channels is imperative. In the second half of this chapter, we will delve deeper into the potential consequences of voyeuristic consumption and examine real-life case studies that shed light on the ethical dilemmas faced by faceless creators. It is through a critical examination of these complexities that we can hope to navigate this digital landscape with empathy, integrity, and a renewed commitment to ethical content creation. Stay tuned for the next chapter, where we unravel the hidden dimensions of faceless YouTube channels and their lasting impact on our society.In the second half of this chapter, we will delve deeper into the potential consequences of voyeuristic consumption and examine real-life case studies that shed light on the ethical dilemmas faced by faceless creators. It is through a critical examination of these complexities that we can hope to navigate this digital landscape with empathy, integrity, and a renewed commitment to ethical content creation.

One of the primary concerns when it comes to consuming faceless YouTube content is the blurred line between entertainment and voyeurism. As viewers, we often find ourselves drawn to these channels out of curiosity and intrigue. However, it is essential to question the impact of our voyeuristic tendencies. By actively participating in the invasion of someone's privacy, we are complicit in potentially harmful consequences. It is crucial for viewers to reflect on their role in perpetuating this voyeuristic culture and to approach faceless YouTube channels with a sense of responsibility and respect for the rights and dignity of the individuals involved.

To further highlight the ethical considerations surrounding faceless YouTube channels, let us explore a few case studies. One example is a popular faceless channel that focuses on documenting the daily lives of unsuspecting individuals. While the content may be enticing to viewers, it raises significant concerns regarding consent. Without obtaining explicit permission to film and publish intimate moments of someone's life, the creators of such channels may be infringing upon their subjects' right to privacy. This case highlights the importance of obtaining consent and respecting boundaries while creating faceless content.

Another case study involves a faceless channel that explores sensitive and personal topics, such as mental health or trauma. While creators may aim to provide a platform for marginalized voices to be heard, it is crucial to assess the potential harm that could arise from revealing private struggles without the subject's explicit consent. It is essential for creators to approach such topics with sensitivity and to prioritize the well-being and privacy of those involved.

Additionally, faceless YouTube channels also expose creators to their own set of ethical dilemmas. They must grapple with the responsibility of maintaining anonymity while ensuring authenticity and transparency. Creators may face challenges in striking the right balance between revealing enough about themselves to establish credibility while still protecting their identity. It is important for faceless content creators to reflect on and navigate these ethical considerations, as they have the power to significantly impact the lives of both themselves and their viewers.

In conclusion, the exploration of ethical considerations surrounding faceless YouTube channels is essential for both creators and viewers. By critically examining the potential consequences and ethical implications, we can work towards responsible content creation and consumption. This requires striking a delicate balance between providing a platform for diverse voices, respecting privacy and consent, and acting with empathy and integrity. As we continue to navigate this digital landscape, let us remember the power we hold as creators and viewers and use it responsibly. By prioritizing ethical content creation, we can ensure that faceless YouTube channels contribute positively to our society.

Chapter 5: Psychology Behind the Viewer-Content Creator Relationship

In the vast realm of YouTube, a peculiar and captivating phenomenon has emerged - the relationship between faceless content creators and their audiences. This unique relationship offers a fascinating glimpse into the intricate workings of human psychology. It delves into the depths of voyeurism, connecting creators and viewers in ways that transcend the boundaries of traditional media.
To truly understand this intriguing dynamic, we must first explore the motives behind both parties. For content creators, anonymity provides a safe haven, a refuge from the judgment and scrutiny that can accompany direct personal exposure. The lack of visibility empowers them to explore their creativity without the constraints of conventional appearances. It allows their content to take center stage, drawing viewers in with a focus solely on the material presented.
On the other side of the screen, audiences are drawn to the mystique surrounding these faceless creators. The absence of physical features encourages viewers to delve deeper into the personality beneath the anonymity. This psychological engagement, often referred to as parasocial interaction, enables individuals to develop one-sided relationships with these content creators, almost as if a genuine connection has been forged.

But what drives individuals to invest their time and emotions into relationships that exist solely through a screen? Research suggests that parasocial interaction serves important psychological needs. It offers a sense of companionship and alleviates feelings of loneliness, particularly in a world where digital connections have become pervasive. By forming attachments to faceless content creators, viewers can derive emotional comfort and a sense of belonging. Beyond companionship, these relationships also tap into the innate human desire for validation and admiration. Viewers often idolize content creators, projecting their own aspirations onto them. The anonymity of these creators allows audiences to focus solely on the content itself, idealizing them as embodiments of their own aspirations and desires. This process is known as symbolic self-completion, where individuals use others as a means to fulfill their unmet needs and aspirations.

As the viewer-content creator relationship deepens, an interconnected web of psychological factors begins to emerge. The power dynamics inherent in these relationships are often reminiscent of traditional media, where the audience passively consumes content. However, within the world of faceless YouTube channels, the boundary between creator and viewer blurs.

Content creators hold a remarkable amount of influence over their audience's emotional states, opinions, and even purchasing habits. Their ability to impact viewers becomes evident through comment sections and messages flooded with praise, criticism, and suggestions. This interplay opens the door for parasocial influencers, where the traditional roles of celebrity and fan merge into an amorphous relationship of mutual influence.

The psychology behind the viewer-content creator relationship is a captivating journey into the human psyche. Understanding the motives, needs, and dynamics at play sheds light on the allure of faceless YouTube channels. As we venture deeper into the second half of this chapter, we will explore the darker implications of this relationship. How does it shape our individual identities and collective society? How does it impact our perceptions of reality and authenticity? Brace yourself as we unveil the hidden forces that lie beneath the surface of YouTube's faceless phenomenon.

The tangled web of the viewer-content creator relationship extends beyond the realm of emotional connection and companionship. It also affects how we perceive reality and authenticity in the digital age. As viewers become increasingly invested in the lives of faceless content creators, a blurred line emerges between the private and public self, leading to questions about authenticity and fabricated personas. In today's age of curated social media feeds and carefully crafted online identities, faceless YouTube channels offer a different perspective. By removing the focus from physical appearances, content creators have the freedom to construct their persona solely around their content. This shift towards content-based identification presents an interesting paradox - on one hand, it allows creators to express themselves more authentically through their work, free from societal judgments based on appearances. Yet, it also raises concerns about the authenticity of the creator's persona itself.

Viewers often develop a deep sense of trust and intimacy with these content creators, which can blur the boundaries between reality and fiction. The parasocial relationship can sometimes lead viewers to believe that they truly know the creators, even though the interaction is purely one-sided. This phenomenon has led to instances where content creators exploit this perceived trust to manipulate their audience's behavior or promote products without proper disclosure. As viewers, we must be mindful of the potential for deception and carefully consider the authenticity of the content presented to us.

Another aspect to consider is the influence that faceless YouTube channels have on our collective society. With millions of subscribers, these channels hold significant power to shape public opinion, trends, and even political narratives. In some cases, the influence of content creators has far-reaching consequences, far beyond the realm of entertainment or personal expression.

The rise of faceless YouTube channels also shines a light on the impact of digital saturation on our perception of reality. We are bombarded with a constant stream of content, which makes it increasingly difficult to discern what is genuine and what is manufactured. The quest for authenticity becomes a challenge in a world where anyone can create a convincing persona behind a screen, blurring the lines between reality and illusion.

Moreover, the viewer-content creator relationship raises concerns about the potential for isolation and social disconnection. As we invest more of our time and emotions into these one-sided relationships, there's a risk of neglecting our real-life connections and engaging in genuine face-to-face interactions. It is crucial to strike a balance between online and offline connections, ensuring that our engagement with faceless YouTube channels doesn't replace genuine human connections.

In conclusion, the viewer-content creator relationship on faceless YouTube channels is a complex interplay of motives, influences, and psychological dynamics. It offers companionship and fulfillment of unmet needs but also poses challenges concerning authenticity and the blurring of reality. As adults navigating the digital landscape, it is essential to critically examine our engagement with these channels and be mindful of the potential implications they may have on our identities, perceptions, and connections with others. Only by understanding these dynamics can we truly appreciate the intriguing and captivating world of faceless YouTube channels and their psychological impact on us as viewers.

Chapter 6: Exploring Different Types of Faceless YouTube Channels

In the vast landscape of YouTube, there exists a peculiar corner of content creators that have managed to captivate audiences without ever revealing their faces. These enigmatic personalities, known as faceless YouTubers, have been gaining traction, and in this chapter, we delve into the various genres and themes that these channels encompass.

One prominent genre found within the realm of faceless YouTube channels is storytelling. These channels enthrall viewers with intricate narratives, weaving tales of mystery, horror, and suspense. The absence of a visible face draws focus to the narrative itself, creating an immersive experience for the audience. Viewers become engrossed in the stories, eagerly anticipating each subsequent episode.

Faceless storytellers skillfully craft their videos with atmospheric sound effects, haunting music, and chilling animations, presenting tales that linger long after the video reaches its conclusion.

However, not all faceless YouTube channels delve into the realm of fiction. Many creators specialize in the art of everyday observation, distinctively capturing moments from ordinary lives. These channels provide a glimpse into the unadorned reality of various individuals, contributing to a unique tapestry of humanity. From channels dedicated to documenting urban exploration, where faceless creators venture into abandoned buildings, to those focused on chronicling the daily routines of people from diverse cultures, these content creators offer an intimate lens through which viewers can explore different lives and perspectives.

One particularly fascinating subset of faceless YouTube channels focuses on providing tutorials and how-to guides, remaining anonymous throughout the instructional process. By avoiding the spotlight on their identities, these creators emphasize the content itself, ensuring that viewers concentrate solely on acquiring new skills and knowledge. From crafting to cooking, these faceless instructors skillfully guide their audience with expert advice, fostering a sense of learning and empowerment.

Additionally, faceless YouTube channels explore a wide range of themes, often pushing the boundaries of conventional content. Some channels explore the world of ASMR, employing various sounds and visual triggers to induce a comforting and relaxing experience for their viewers. Others delve into the mysterious realm of conspiracy theories, analyzing evidence and presenting their findings without revealing their identities, allowing viewers to discern the truth for themselves.

As we continue to examine the world of faceless YouTube channels, it becomes apparent that this unconventional approach to content creation has captured the attention and admiration of countless individuals. These channels transcend the need for personal appearance, focusing instead on the power of storytelling, observation, education, and exploration. The diverse genres and themes encompassed within the realm of faceless YouTube channels provide a testament to the boundless creativity and ingenuity of its creators. From the allure of captivating narratives to the immersive experience of observing everyday lives, these channels offer a wealth of entertainment, knowledge, and thought-provoking content.

But what lies beneath the surface of these captivating channels? How do faceless YouTubers navigate the complexities of online anonymity while resonating deeply with their audiences? In the second half of this chapter, we shall embark on a journey of discovery, peeling back the layers of faceless YouTube channels to expose the motivations, challenges, and secrets that lie within their masked identities.

Stay tuned for the second half, where we unlock the secrets behind the mask and explore the fascinating world of faceless YouTubers. Within the realm of faceless YouTube channels, there exists a veil of secrecy and anonymity that adds an intriguing layer to the content being produced. As we delve deeper into this captivating world, it is essential to uncover the motivations, challenges, and secrets that lie behind the masked identities of faceless YouTubers.

For these creators, anonymity provides a unique freedom to explore their passions without the constraints of personal image or public scrutiny. It allows them to focus solely on their content, enabling a more authentic and uninhibited creative process. Through their faceless personas, they can channel their creativity and expertise directly into the videos they produce, unburdened by concerns of personal appearance or judgment.

Yet, navigating the complexities of online anonymity comes with its own set of challenges. Faceless YouTubers must carefully balance their desired level of anonymity with their desire to connect with their audience. They must develop distinct identities and captivating content that resonates with viewers without relying on the visual cues typically associated with a persona.

These creators often rely on other elements, such as voice modulation, unique editing styles, or the use of avatars or animations, to establish a recognizable presence and forge a connection with their audience. By honing these techniques, faceless YouTubers are able to cultivate a loyal following based solely on the quality and appeal of their content.

Furthermore, the concept of faceless YouTube channels invites speculation and curiosity. Viewers are left wondering about the individuals behind the mask and what drives them to create such captivating content. This mystery creates an aura of intrigue, drawing audiences in and encouraging them to delve deeper into the stories and videos being presented.

In some cases, the anonymous nature of faceless YouTube channels also serves as a form of protection for the creators. It shields them from potential backlash, privacy invasion, or harassment that can often follow those who reveal their identities online. This anonymity allows the creators to fearlessly explore controversial or sensitive topics, pushing the boundaries of conventional content and raising thought-provoking questions without fear of personal repercussions.

Faceless YouTube channels have carved out a unique niche within the vast landscape of online content creation. They offer a refreshing alternative to the heavily saturated realm of personality-driven media. By removing the focus from the individual creator, these channels encourage viewers to engage solely with the content itself, fostering a deeper appreciation for the stories, knowledge, and experiences being shared.

As we conclude our deep dive into the world of faceless YouTube channels, it becomes evident that these creators are true trailblazers in the realm of online entertainment and education. Their dedication to their craft, their ability to captivate and connect with audiences, and their willingness to explore unconventional themes and genres are all testaments to their boundless creativity and ingenuity.

In the realm of faceless YouTube channels, the power of storytelling, observation, education, and exploration transcends personal identities. It is a testament to the endless possibilities of content creation and the impact that can be made when individuals are liberated from the constraints of personal appearance. As we bid farewell to this chapter, let us continue to embrace the journey of discovery, appreciating the depth and richness that faceless YouTube channels bring to our screens.

Chapter 7: Entertainment vs. Invasion of Privacy

Weighing the thin line between entertainment and invading personal boundaries, it becomes crucial to question the extent to which faceless YouTube channels cross that line. In a digital era where content creation is at its peak, these platforms have given rise to a new form of entertainment, captivating millions of viewers worldwide. However, this phenomenon isn't without its controversies, as the boundaries of privacy become blurred in the pursuit of online engagement. Faceless YouTube channels, characterized by creators who choose not to reveal their identities, often attract millions of subscribers. These content creators produce a wide range of videos, including commentary, reactions, and even pranks. At first glance, their content appears harmless, providing endless entertainment and an escape from the monotony of everyday life. Yet, as we delve deeper into their methods, it raises the question of whether they are crossing the line between entertainment and invading personal privacy.

One of the most concerning aspects is the creation of content that includes unsuspecting individuals without their consent. We've all seen videos where random people in public spaces are approached and put on the spot, often causing discomfort or embarrassment. Creators argue that their intentions are harmless, purely aiming to capture genuine reactions for entertainment purposes. However, critics argue that these faceless YouTube channels exploit vulnerable individuals for their own gain, disregarding the impact on the subjects' emotional well-being.

Another form of invasion of privacy is the exploitation of personal information. Some faceless YouTube channels investigate personal accounts, scouring the web for intimate details to share with their audience. While creators may justify their actions by arguing that the information is publicly available, the ethical implications arise when they delve into the private lives of individuals without their consent. This raises important questions about the boundaries between entertainment and the right to privacy.

Aside from the direct impact on individuals, these faceless YouTube channels also raise concerns about the potential normalization of voyeuristic behavior. As more and more people consume this content, viewers unknowingly become complicit in the invasion of privacy. By rewarding these creators with views and engagement, we inadvertently condone the violation of personal boundaries. The power dynamic between creators and their audience becomes skewed, and the potential harm caused cannot be ignored.

As we continue to navigate the ever-evolving landscape of online entertainment, it is vital to critically examine the impact and ethical implications of faceless YouTube channels. While the allure of voyeurism and the thrill of unmasking secrets may captivate audiences, we must also consider the potential harm caused to those who unknowingly become part of this content. The line between entertainment and invasion of privacy remains delicate, and it is essential for society to actively engage in discussions that hold creators accountable for their actions.

Suspense hangs in the air as we explore the second half of this chapter, where we delve further into the consequences, potential solutions, and the role of individuals and platforms in balancing entertainment and personal boundaries. Without a clear conclusion, we invite you to ponder these questions: How can we find a balance that respects personal privacy without stifling creativity and expression? What responsibility should these faceless YouTube channels bear? Join us as we uncover the complexities within this ever-growing digital phenomenon. In the pursuit of finding a delicate balance between entertainment and the invasion of personal boundaries, it is crucial to delve deeper into the consequences and potential solutions surrounding faceless YouTube channels. As the popularity of these channels grows, so does the need for individuals and platforms to take responsibility for the impact of their content.

The consequences of crossing the line between entertainment and invasion of privacy can be far-reaching. For the unsuspecting individuals featured in these videos, the emotional toll can be significant. Being targeted in public spaces without consent can lead to feelings of discomfort, embarrassment, and even distress. The long-lasting effects of such experiences cannot be dismissed, as they have the potential to damage not only the emotional well-being of the individuals involved but also their trust in others.

Furthermore, the exploitation of personal information by faceless YouTube channels sets a troubling precedent. While some creators argue that the information they share is publicly available, the moral implications arise when personal lives are invaded without consent. It is essential to recognize the right to privacy and question whether the desire for entertainment outweighs the ethical responsibility to protect individuals' personal boundaries.

As we navigate this complex landscape, potential solutions come into focus. Firstly, it is crucial for platforms to establish clear guidelines and policies regarding privacy. By enforcing stricter regulations and monitoring content more closely, platforms can ensure that creators are held accountable for their actions. Encouraging responsible content creation that respects personal privacy should be a priority. Additionally, creators themselves need to take a more thoughtful and considerate approach when producing their videos. By incorporating consent into their content creation process, they can strike a balance between entertainment and personal boundaries. Seeking consent from individuals before featuring them in videos or refraining from the exploitation of personal information are simple yet powerful steps that can greatly mitigate the invasion of privacy. Lastly, the responsibility lies not only on platforms and creators but also on the audience. As viewers, we have the power to shape the narrative by supporting content that values personal privacy and ethical practices. By becoming more discerning consumers, actively engaging in discussions, and providing feedback, we can drive positive change in the digital landscape.

In conclusion, the allure of faceless YouTube channels and their entertainment value cannot be denied. However, it is essential to critically examine the consequences and ethical implications that arise when personal boundaries are crossed. Through clear guidelines and policies, responsible content creation, and active engagement from both platforms and viewers, we can find a balance that respects personal privacy without stifling creativity and expression. It is time for society to hold faceless YouTube channels accountable and promote a digital environment that values personal boundaries and ethical practices. Only then can we ensure that the line between entertainment and invasion of privacy is delicately upheld for the betterment of all.

Chapter 8: Legal Implications and Regulations in Faceless YouTube Content

As the popularity of faceless YouTube channels continues to rise, it becomes crucial to navigate the legal landscape surrounding this unique genre of content. With their anonymous creators and captivating yet enigmatic videos, faceless channels pose various legal implications and raise questions about the boundaries of privacy, consent, and intellectual property rights.

One of the primary legal concerns surrounding faceless YouTube content is privacy. While many creators blur or alter their faces to conceal their identity, it remains essential for them to respect the privacy of others appearing in their videos. Consent plays a pivotal role here, as creators must obtain permission from individuals before featuring them in their content, especially when it involves sensitive or personal topics. Failure to do so may result in legal consequences, including invasion of privacy claims or even potential lawsuits.

Furthermore, faceless channels often delve into public spaces, where individuals with no relation to the content may inadvertently appear. In such cases, content creators must be cautious not to exploit or harass unknowing participants. Respect for personal boundaries and ethical considerations are necessary to ensure that the content remains within legal limits.

Intellectual property is another aspect that faceless YouTube creators must be aware of. Utilizing copyrighted material without obtaining proper permissions or licenses can potentially lead to copyright infringement claims. Fair use of copyrighted materials, such as brief snippets for commentary or criticism, might be permissible under certain circumstances. However, it is crucial for creators to understand the intricacies of copyright laws to avoid legal entanglements.

Moreover, there is an ongoing debate regarding the liability of faceless YouTube channels for the actions of their audience. While creators can control the content they produce, they may not have direct control over how viewers interpret or use their videos. However, if the content encourages illegal or harmful activities, creators may be held liable to some extent. Clear disclaimers, moderation efforts, and an understanding of community guidelines can help provide protection against potential legal repercussions arising from viewer actions.

As the faceless YouTube phenomenon evolves, regulations are starting to catch up with this unique form of content creation. Some countries have already introduced legislation that regulates online content and user-generated media, aiming to strike a balance between freedom of expression and protection of rights. However, implementing and enforcing such regulations can be challenging due to the global nature of YouTube and the diverse legal frameworks across different jurisdictions.

While faceless YouTube content has undoubtedly captured the attention of millions worldwide, the legal implications surrounding it cannot be overlooked. Creators must navigate the complex web of privacy, consent, intellectual property, and potential liability to ensure their content remains both captivating and legally compliant. As we explore the legal landscape surrounding faceless YouTube channels, it becomes evident that every video uploaded holds potential legal consequences, making it crucial for creators to tread carefully in this enigmatic realm of online content. Furthermore, faceless YouTube channels have also sparked debates regarding the intersection of free speech and potential harm caused by their content. While creators have the right to express themselves, they must be conscious of the potential consequences that their actions may have on others. This includes being aware of hate speech, offensive language, or the incitement of violence in their videos, which can lead to legal issues and public backlash.

Creators of faceless YouTube channels should understand that their freedom of expression is not absolute and may be subject to legal limitations. Many countries have laws in place to regulate and restrict certain types of speech, such as defamation, hate speech, or obscenity. It is the responsibility of content creators to familiarize themselves with these laws and ensure that their content aligns with legal standards. Moreover, creators must also consider the potential impact their videos may have on vulnerable or impressionable viewers. Content that promotes dangerous or harmful behaviors, such as self-harm or suicide, can have severe consequences on individuals who may be influenced by what they see. In such cases, creators may face legal repercussions if their content is proven to have contributed to the harm or endangerment of others.

To mitigate these risks, content creators should be proactive in implementing moderation efforts and community guidelines. Clear disclaimers that outline the purpose and nature of their content, along with guidance on responsible viewing, can help protect creators against potential legal liabilities arising from audience actions. Additionally, actively monitoring and promptly removing any comments or content that violate community guidelines can help ensure a safe and responsible viewing environment.

As faceless YouTube content gains more traction, legislators worldwide are grappling with the task of regulating this unique genre of content. Some countries have introduced legislation aimed at combating online harassment, protecting user privacy, and addressing issues surrounding anonymity. These regulations seek to strike a balance between safeguarding individual rights and promoting a respectful and responsible online environment. However, enforcing such regulations poses significant challenges due to the global nature of YouTube and the varying legal frameworks across different jurisdictions. The internet knows no physical boundaries, and content creators may find themselves navigating a patchwork of laws and regulations as their videos reach audiences worldwide. This highlights the need for greater international cooperation and harmonization of legal standards in relation to faceless YouTube content.

In conclusion, faceless YouTube channels present a myriad of legal implications and regulations that content creators must navigate. Privacy, consent, intellectual property, potential liability, and the intersection of free speech and harm are all crucial considerations in this realm. As legislation continues to evolve, creators must stay informed and adapt their practices to ensure they remain within legal boundaries.

With millions of viewers consuming faceless YouTube content, creators hold a significant responsibility to uphold ethical and legal standards. By respecting privacy, obtaining consent, understanding intellectual property laws, and being mindful of their influence, creators can continue to captivate audiences while avoiding legal consequences. As adults, it is essential for us to be aware of these intricacies and engage in thoughtful discussions surrounding the legal landscape of faceless YouTube channels.

Chapter 9: Case Studies: Success and Controversies

In the ever-evolving realm of YouTube, a plethora of unique content creators have emerged over the years, captivating audiences with their faceless personas. These enigmatic channels have sparked intrigue and fascination, raising questions about the impact of this phenomenon. In this chapter, we will delve into the success stories and controversies surrounding notable faceless YouTube channels, hoping to gain valuable insights into their influence and enduring popularity. One such channel that demands attention is the enigmatic "Mystique Chronicles." This channel, shrouded in anonymity, specializes in narrating mysterious tales, blending elements of horror, suspense, and the supernatural. With its spine-chilling stories and skilled storytelling, Mystique Chronicles has garnered a massive following of devoted fans eager for a nightly dose of chilling narratives. The channel's meticulously crafted videos, accompanied by eerie background music, create an immersive experience that keeps viewers on the edge of their seats. Blurring the line between reality and fiction, Mystique Chronicles has seamlessly woven itself into the tapestry of YouTube's faceless wonders.

While Mystique Chronicles represents the pinnacle of success, not all faceless YouTube channels have smooth sailing. The channel "Controversy Unleashed" embodies the flip side of this phenomenon, as it has faced its fair share of challenges. Operating on the principles of investigative journalism, Controversy Unleashed has plagued the internet with exposes, unmasking the shady dealings of individuals and organizations. However, its quest for truth has often landed the channel in hot water, facing legal threats and intense backlash from those exposed. Controversy Unleashed raises important ethical questions about the fine line between journalistic integrity and privacy invasion, stirring a heated debate among its followers and the wider YouTube community.

Moving on to brighter horizons, the channel "Artful Expressions" serves as a testament to the transformative power of art. Through mesmerizing time-lapses of intricate sketches and captivating paintings, Artful Expressions showcases the artistic talents of a faceless artist. Its videos, accompanied by calming music, provide a therapeutic escape for viewers, allowing them to witness the birth of awe-inspiring creations. The channel's success lies not only in the artistic prowess displayed but also in its ability to foster a sense of serenity and inspiration amidst the chaos of daily life.

As we examine these case studies, it becomes evident that faceless YouTube channels have permeated various genres and captured the hearts and minds of viewers worldwide. They have carved a niche for themselves in the digital landscape, revolutionizing the way we consume content. These channels have adeptly harnessed the power of anonymity, drawing viewers in with their unique storytelling styles, investigative pursuits, or artistic endeavors.

But what drives the success and controversies surrounding these enigmatic creators? Is it their ability to tap into our unexplored fears? Are the controversies a consequence of their relentless pursuit of truth? Or is it simply the allure of the unknown that keeps audiences coming back for more? In the second half of this chapter, we will continue to unveil the secrets behind their triumphs and challenges. We will unravel the complexities surrounding faceless YouTube channels, exploring the psychological and societal factors that contribute to their impact.

Stay tuned, as we embark on a journey that reveals the captivating world behind faceless YouTube channels, exposing the triumphs and controversies that define this phenomenon. In the second half of this chapter, we will continue our exploration of faceless YouTube channels, uncovering more intriguing case studies that shed light on the essence of their success and the controversies they attract. We will delve deeper into the psychological and societal factors that contribute to the impact of these enigmatic creators, fostering an understanding of their enduring popularity.

One notable faceless YouTube channel that has gained significant recognition is "Tech Secrets Unveiled." This channel focuses on dissecting the inner workings of technology, providing viewers with tutorials, reviews, and insider information. By donning a faceless persona, Tech Secrets Unveiled maintains a level of anonymity that sparks curiosity and adds an air of mystery to their content. Their expertise and concise explanations have attracted a vast community of tech enthusiasts who eagerly follow their videos for the latest updates and insights. However, the channel's success has not come without controversy. Some argue that their anonymous approach raises questions about accountability and credibility, fueling debates within the tech community regarding the trade-offs between disclosure and expertise.

Another intriguing case study is the channel "Voices Unheard." With a focus on storytelling, this faceless YouTube channel gives voice to marginalized communities and raises awareness about social issues. By concealing their identity and allowing the stories to take center stage, Voices Unheard has created a safe space for people to share their experiences and perspectives. The channel's impact lies not only in the captivating narratives but also in the empathy and compassion it fosters among its viewers. However, the channel has faced criticism for potentially exploiting sensitive stories for views and failing to ensure the full consent and well-being of the individuals involved. This controversy highlights the delicate balance between giving voice to the voiceless and respecting the boundaries of privacy.

Moving on, we encounter the channel "Empowering Entrepreneurship." This faceless YouTube channel focuses on providing guidance, inspiration, and practical advice for aspiring entrepreneurs. The anonymity of the creator allows the channel to transcend personal identity and focus solely on empowering its audience. By drawing attention to the stories and journeys of successful entrepreneurs, Empowering Entrepreneurship creates a sense of universality and encourages viewers to pursue their dreams. However, the channel's success has attracted the attention of skeptics who question the credibility of faceless mentors, as transparency is often associated with trust in the business world. The controversies surrounding Empowering Entrepreneurship prompt us to consider whether anonymity enables a broader reach or if it compromises the authenticity of the advice offered. As we examine these case studies, it becomes increasingly clear that the success and controversies surrounding faceless YouTube channels are complex and multifaceted. From the allure of anonymity to the ethical implications of privacy invasion, from the universal appeal of storytelling to the concerns of credibility, these enigmatic creators navigate a delicate balance between capturing audiences and facing criticism.

In conclusion, faceless YouTube channels have transformed the way we consume content, captivating audiences worldwide with their unique storytelling styles, investigative pursuits, and artistic endeavors. The success and controversies they attract are a reflection of the impact they have on our society. By understanding the psychological and societal factors at play, we can better grasp the allure of the unknown and the triumphs and challenges that define this phenomenon.

Join us on this captivating journey through the captivating world of faceless YouTube channels, as we delve into the intricacies and unravel the secrets behind their influence and enduring popularity.

_____

Chapter 10: The Role of Social Media and Online Communities

In this digital age, social media and online communities play a profound role in shaping our lives and the way we consume content. When it comes to the realm of faceless YouTube channels, the influence of these platforms becomes even more evident. Throughout this chapter, we will investigate the impact of social media and online communities in supporting, discussing, and spreading the content created by faceless YouTube channels.

One cannot deny the power of social media in amplifying the reach of faceless YouTube channels. Platforms such as Twitter, Facebook, and Instagram serve as virtual meeting grounds for fans and followers to come together, share their opinions, and build communities around their favorite channels. Hashtags dedicated to specific channels trend worldwide, allowing users to easily access and engage with the content. Through retweets, shares, and tags, the content spreads like wildfire, reaching audiences far beyond the initial subscriber count.

The connection between social media and faceless YouTube channels has also given rise to a new breed of content creators—referred to as "reaction channels." These channels take the content of faceless YouTubers and provide commentary, reactions, and analysis. It's through this collaborative relationship that the content gains further exposure and a broader perspective is offered to viewers. These reaction channels not only generate discussions within their own communities but also contribute to the overall growth and popularity of the faceless YouTube genre.

Online communities centered around faceless YouTube channels serve as digital gathering spaces where fans can bond over shared interests and fuel their curiosity. These communities provide a sense of belonging and a platform for individuals to exchange theories, interpretations, and even criticism of the content. The support within these communities helps to create a highly engaged audience, dedicated to exploring the depths of the faceless YouTube channel's content. It is within these communities that new ideas are generated, debates are sparked, and the content is examined from multiple perspectives.

Furthermore, social media platforms and online communities have played a significant role in the rise of mini-influencers within the faceless YouTube realm. These are individuals who gain recognition and a loyal following by analyzing, dissecting, or reimagining the content. Through their own unique interpretations, mini-influencers contribute to the ongoing conversations surrounding faceless YouTube channels. They craft their own narratives, theories, and even alternate storylines, captivating audiences with their creative take on the content. By doing so, they not only add to the tapestry of the channel's universe but also generate further curiosity and engagement from viewers.

As we delve deeper into the realms of social media and online communities, the symbiotic relationship between faceless YouTube channels and these platforms becomes increasingly apparent. The interconnectedness of these elements creates a web of engagement that fuels the content's popularity, encourages discussion, and nurtures a sense of community among viewers. However, the influence of social media and online communities does not come without its challenges and potential downsides. In the second half of this chapter, we will explore the darker side of this relationship and its implications for both content creators and viewers alike.

(End of first half with a sentence to be continued...)Online communities and social media platforms have undeniably revolutionized the way we consume content and engage with our favorite faceless YouTube channels. However, this symbiotic relationship between technology and content creation also comes with its fair share of challenges and potential downsides.

One of the inherent risks of the digital age is the rapid spread of misinformation. Social media platforms and online communities can inadvertently contribute to the spread of rumors, conspiracy theories, and false narratives surrounding faceless YouTube channels. As information spreads like wildfire through shares and retweets, it becomes increasingly difficult to discern fact from fiction. This not only creates confusion among viewers but also poses a potential threat to the credibility of the content itself.

Furthermore, the constant demand for new, engaging content in the fast-paced realm of social media can put immense pressure on faceless YouTube creators. The need to continuously produce fresh material can lead to burnout and a decline in the quality of content. This, coupled with the pressure to keep up with trends, can dilute the originality and authentic voice of the channels. As a result, creators may struggle to strike a balance between maintaining their integrity and appeasing the demands of their audience.

Another concern arises from the monetization of YouTube channels through sponsorships and brand deals. While these partnerships can provide financial stability for content creators, they also present ethical challenges. The integration of sponsored content within faceless YouTube channels may blur the line between organic content and promotional material, compromising the trust between creators and viewers. It is crucial for content creators to transparently disclose their partnerships to maintain the authenticity and integrity of their channels.

Additionally, the anonymity of online communities can foster a toxic culture of harassment and hate speech. While social media platforms have implemented measures to combat online bullying, the anonymous nature of the internet still allows for the proliferation of negative behavior. Faceless YouTube channels and their creators are not immune to the clutches of online harassment, with individuals hiding behind their screens to spread vitriol and negativity. This toxic environment can create a hostile space for both content creators and viewers, eroding the sense of community that should ideally be fostered.

Despite these challenges, the influence of social media and online communities on faceless YouTube channels cannot be denied. The power of these platforms in amplifying content, fostering discussion, and nurturing communities remains a prominent force in the digital age. However, it is the responsibility of both viewers and creators to navigate this relationship mindfully and ethically, fostering a healthy and respectful online environment.

In conclusion, the impact of social media and online communities on faceless YouTube channels is undeniable. While these platforms offer immense opportunities for engagement and growth, they also come with their fair share of challenges. By recognizing the potential downsides and actively addressing them, content creators and viewers can ensure that the symbiotic relationship between social media, online communities, and faceless YouTube channels remains a positive force in shaping the landscape of digital content creation.

Chapter 11: The Future of Faceless YouTube Channels

Speculate and forecast the trends and potential developments awaiting faceless YouTube channels in the future.

In recent years, faceless YouTube channels have revolutionized the way we consume content online. These channels, run by anonymous individuals who prefer to remain hidden behind masks or avatars, have captivated audiences with their unique approach to storytelling and captivating visuals. As we venture into the future, it is fascinating to speculate on the potential trends and developments that await these faceless creators.

One prominent trend that can be expected is the continued blurring of the line between reality and fiction. Faceless YouTube channels thrive on creating alternate realities and engaging narratives, leaving viewers questioning the authenticity of what they see. In the future, this trend is likely to intensify as creators find innovative ways to immerse their audience even further. Virtual reality technology may play a crucial role in this, allowing viewers to step into the world of these channels and experience their stories firsthand.

Another potential development is the expansion of faceless YouTube channels into different genres and niches. Currently, we primarily see these channels in the realm of horror and mystery, where their anonymity adds an extra layer of suspense. However, as viewers become more accustomed to this storytelling style, expect to see them branching out into other genres such as comedy, drama, or even educational content. Their unique approach to storytelling can breathe new life into these genres, attracting a wide range of viewers.

Furthermore, the future holds the promise of increased collaboration among faceless YouTube channels. As the popularity of these channels grows, creators may come together to collaborate on large-scale projects, pooling their resources and talents to create truly immersive experiences. These collaborations could involve intricate crossovers, where characters from different channels intertwine in a shared universe. Such collaborations would undoubtedly generate heightened audience anticipation and excitement.

In addition to collaboration, faceless YouTube channels might leverage emerging technologies, such as artificial intelligence, to further enhance their content creation. AI-powered algorithms could analyze viewers' preferences, allowing creators to tailor their stories and videos to specific individuals. This personalized approach would deepen viewer engagement and strengthen the bond between the channel and its audience.

One cannot discuss the future of faceless YouTube channels without considering the potential impact of ethical and legal concerns. As these channels gain prominence, questions surrounding privacy, consent, and the potential for harm may arise. Regulations may be put in place to protect both creators and viewers, ensuring responsible content production and consumption. These developments could shape the future landscape of faceless YouTube channels, demanding accountability and transparency from their creators.

As we come to the end of this first half, it becomes evident that faceless YouTube channels are set to evolve and push the boundaries of online content creation in the future. From blurring reality and fiction to genre expansion, collaboration, and ethical considerations, the possibilities for these channels are vast. The second half of this chapter will delve deeper into these exciting prospects and reveal further insights into the future of faceless YouTube channels. Stay tuned for the next part, where we continue this captivating journey into the unknown. In the ever-evolving landscape of faceless YouTube channels, one can anticipate a plethora of intriguing developments that will shape the future of content creation. This second half of the chapter will continue our exploration of the exciting prospects awaiting these channels and shed light on further insights into their future.

One notable aspect that is likely to emerge in the future is the incorporation of interactive elements within faceless YouTube channels. As technology advances, creators will find innovative ways to engage their audiences by allowing them to actively participate in the storytelling process. Viewers may be presented with choices and decisions that directly impact the course of the narrative, creating a truly immersive and personalized experience. This level of interactivity will further blur the line between creator and audience, forging a deeper connection that goes beyond mere passive consumption.

As faceless YouTube channels continue to expand into different genres, one can expect creators to experiment with new formats and storytelling techniques. For instance, animation could be utilized to bring their narratives to life, providing a unique visual experience that complements the anonymity of the creators. Additionally, as educational content gains popularity, faceless channels might delve into a realm of thought-provoking and informative videos, utilizing their storytelling prowess to engage and educate audiences on a wide range of subjects.

In a world where viral challenges and trends dominate online platforms, faceless YouTube channels may serve as a powerful tool for promoting important social causes. Creators could utilize their platforms to shed light on pressing issues and initiate meaningful discussions. By tackling topics such as mental health, social justice, and environmental sustainability, these channels can contribute to a more informed and compassionate online community.

While collaboration among faceless YouTube channels has been mentioned in the previous section, it is worth exploring the potential impact this could have on the medium as a whole. As creators join forces, they can harness their collective creativity and diverse perspectives to craft even more engaging and complex narratives. Collaborations between faceless channels could become highly anticipated events, drawing large audiences and generating excitement across various online platforms.

However, amidst the excitement of these future possibilities, it is essential to address the ethical considerations that come with such growth. With increased prominence, faceless YouTube channels may face intensified scrutiny regarding privacy, consent, and the potential for harm. Creators and platform administrators will need to carefully navigate these concerns, ensuring responsible content creation and fostering a safe and inclusive environment for both creators and viewers.

In summary, the future of faceless YouTube channels is full of promise, innovation, and challenges. From interactive storytelling to genre expansion, educational content, and collaborations, the possibilities for these channels are vast. As creators continue to push the boundaries of online content creation, it is crucial to remain vigilant about ethical considerations and the well-being of all involved. Together, creators and viewers can shape a future where faceless YouTube channels thrive as a captivating and responsible medium of expression. So, brace yourselves for a captivating journey into the unknown as the faceless YouTube channels of tomorrow unfold before our eyes.

Chapter 12: The Impact on Audiences and Creators

Reflecting on the broader impact of faceless YouTube channels on both viewers and content creators allows us to delve into the complex implications they have on society as a whole. These enigmatic channels, where creators remain anonymous or hide their faces behind masks and avatars, have surged in popularity, captivating audiences around the world. In this chapter, we will explore the effects experienced by both viewers and creators in this unique digital landscape.

For audiences, faceless YouTube channels offer a peculiar blend of intrigue and mystery. The anonymity of the creator adds an element of suspense and curiosity, enticing viewers to delve deeper into their content. Whether it's unboxing videos, conspiracy theories, or anonymous storytelling, these channels often hold a hypnotic power over their audience, drawing them into a world where the focus is solely on the content being presented. The absence of a visible persona enables viewers to purely focus on the ideas and concepts being shared, unencumbered by biases related to the creator's appearance or personal history.

However, this captivating allure can also raise concerns. Faceless YouTube channels have the potential to blur the lines between reality and fiction, challenging viewers to discern what is genuine and what is fabricated. The anonymity of the creators can lend an air of secrecy to the content, leaving viewers to question the authenticity and intentions behind the videos they consume. This gray area can stir a blend of fascination, skepticism, and even paranoia among audiences as they navigate the uncharted territory of faceless YouTube channels.

For the creators behind these enigmatic channels, the anonymity serves as a double-edged sword. On the one hand, it grants them the freedom to express themselves without the concern of personal judgment or scrutiny. By obscuring their identity, creators can focus solely on their content, allowing their ideas to take center stage. This liberating anonymity enables individuals who may otherwise hesitate to share their thoughts or talents to step forward, contributing to the vast tapestry of knowledge and creativity found on YouTube.

Yet, this anonymity also carries its own set of challenges. Faceless creators must grapple with the notion that their work will be judged solely on its merit, devoid of personal connections or preconceived notions linked to their appearance or background. This pressure to continuously generate captivating content while preserving their anonymity can lead to a perpetual cycle of reinvention, as creators strive to captivate and maintain their audience's attention without the leveraging the traditional methods of personal branding.

With the continual rise of faceless YouTube channels, society is confronted with a new form of media consumption and creation. The impact on both viewers and creators is multifaceted, ranging from a sense of curiosity, skepticism, and fascination for audiences to a freedom of expression paired with the challenges of sustaining anonymity for creators. As we navigate this uncharted terrain, it is crucial to examine the implications wrought by these faceless channels, delving deeper into their influence on our perception of reality, our trust in digital content, and the ever-evolving nature of creativity and entertainment in the digital age.

In examining the impact of faceless YouTube channels on audiences and creators, it is essential to consider the potential effects on the viewers' perception of reality. These enigmatic channels, with their mysterious creators and content, often blur the lines between fact and fiction. As viewers dive deeper into the realm of faceless YouTube channels, they must confront the challenge of discerning what is genuine and what is fabricated. One notable consequence of this blurred reality is the emergence of a new form of skepticism among audiences. As viewers become more engrossed in the captivating allure of faceless channels, they grapple with the inherent paradox of anonymity and authenticity. The absence of a visible persona raises questions about the credibility of the content being presented. Is it truly based on actual experiences and knowledge, or is it an elaborate narrative crafted for entertainment purposes? This delicate balance between fascination and doubt can lead viewers to approach faceless YouTube channels with a heightened sense of scrutiny, questioning every detail and motive behind the content they consume. Moreover, faceless YouTube channels have the power to shape the viewers' trust in digital content. In an era where misinformation and fake news abound, the anonymity of creators can foster a sense of uncertainty and skepticism towards the authenticity of online information. By concealing their identities, faceless creators add an additional layer of complexity to the viewers' ability to discern truth from falsehood. Consequently, audience members may find themselves increasingly cautious when engaging with content from these channels, applying extra scrutiny and fact-checking to ensure they are not being misled.

While viewers grapple with the implications of faceless YouTube channels, the creators themselves also face unique challenges in sustaining their anonymity. In the pursuit of captivating content, these creators must continually reinvent themselves without relying on traditional methods of personal branding. This perpetual cycle of reinvention can be demanding and exhausting, requiring constant innovation and creativity to maintain the audience's attention. It is a delicate balance that pushes faceless creators to focus solely on the quality of their content while ensuring their identities remain hidden—a task requiring immense dedication and adaptability.

The expansion of faceless YouTube channels marks a transformative shift in media consumption and creation. As society continues to navigate this uncharted terrain, it is essential to consider the broader implications these channels have on our perceptions of reality, our trust in digital content, and the evolving nature of creativity and entertainment in the digital age. The impact on both viewers and creators is multifaceted, encompassing curiosity, skepticism, and fascination. By acknowledging these complex dynamics, we can begin to unravel the intricate relationship between faceless YouTube channels, society, and the ever-evolving digital landscape that shapes our lives.

In conclusion, the rise of faceless YouTube channels has engendered both fascination and skepticism among viewers while presenting a unique set of challenges for creators. The blurred lines between reality and fiction demand heightened scrutiny from audiences, distinguishing genuine content from fabricated narratives. Simultaneously, faceless creators strive to maintain their anonymity while continuously generating captivating content, navigating the pressures of reinvention and establishing trust in an age of skepticism. As we delve deeper into the impact of faceless YouTube channels, it becomes clear that this novel form of media consumption and creation marks a pivotal moment for society, shaping our perception of reality and challenging our trust in digital content.

Dear Reader,

I want to extend my heartfelt thanks to you for taking the time to read this book. Your curiosity and willingness to explore the ideas and insights within these pages mean the world to me.

Writing a book is a journey of passion and dedication, and it's readers like you who make that journey truly meaningful. Whether you were seeking knowledge, inspiration, or simply a good story, your decision to pick up this book is a testament to your thirst for understanding and growth.

I hope that the words you've found within these pages have been enlightening, empowering, and, most importantly, enjoyable. Books have a unique ability to transport us to different worlds, challenge our perspectives, and enrich our lives, and it's my sincere hope that this book has done just that for you.

As an author, I am profoundly grateful for the opportunity to share my thoughts and ideas with you. Your support and engagement mean more than words can express. Please know that your time and attention are cherished, and your feedback, if you choose to share it, is invaluable.

Thank you once again for embarking on this literary journey with me. May the knowledge gained from these pages continue to inspire and guide you in your own journey through life.

With deepest gratitude,

Ben Davis

Thankyou

Thank you for your purchase! If you enjoyed this book, please consider dropping me a review. It take 5 seconds and helps a small business like mine.

www.ingramcontent.com/pod-product-compliance
Lightning Source LLC
Chambersburg PA
CBHW061051050326
40690CB00012B/2575